Clean Up C...

Ride Bikes, Not Cars!

We Need New Playground Equipment!

THREE PERSUASIVE LETTERS

by Cynthia Swain

Table of Contents

Persuasive Letters

What is a persuasive letter?

A persuasive letter is a letter that tries to convince readers to believe or do something. A persuasive letter has a strong point of view about an idea or a problem. It includes facts and examples to support an opinion, and it usually suggests a solution.

What is the purpose of a persuasive letter?

People write persuasive letters to "sway," or change the minds of, their readers. They want readers to see their points of view. They may want readers to take action, too.

Who is the audience for persuasive letters?

People write persuasive letters to all kinds of people: parents, friends, citizens, business leaders, world leaders, and others. They write letters to make people understand their views. Often they want to change their audience's opinions. For example, someone might write to a leader about a law they don't agree with. The writer might want the leader to change the law.

How do you read a persuasive letter?

Keep in mind that the writer wants you to support his or her position. Ask yourself, *What is this writer's position, or opinion? Does she support it with facts and good reasons? Do I agree with her?* A good persuasive writer knows her audience. She knows what facts and reasons might change her reader's mind.

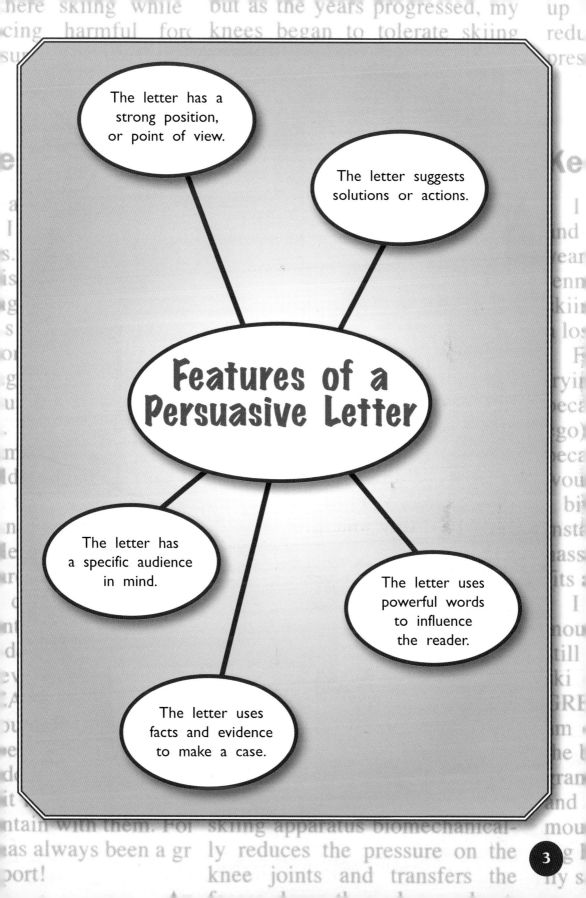

The letter has a strong position, or point of view.

The letter suggests solutions or actions.

Features of a Persuasive Letter

The letter has a specific audience in mind.

The letter uses powerful words to influence the reader.

The letter uses facts and evidence to make a case.

Letters That Made a Difference

A letter can change a person's mind. Some letters can even help change the world. People have been writing letters for centuries. Here is one example of a letter writer who made a difference.

Jane Goodall

Jane Goodall is a famous scientist. She studied chimps in Africa for many years. Then she started a group to protect animals and the environment. She has written many letters. She has written letters to people all around the world.

In one letter, Goodall wrote about animal research. She wanted people to think about whether or not to allow animal research. She said, "I am writing to you on behalf of the millions of animals each year who are subjects of laboratory experiments . . ." She asked people to hold meetings about the issue. She wanted them to learn more about what was being done to animals.

In another letter, Goodall wrote about the danger of plastic bags. She supported her position with facts. "The Environmental Protection Agency estimates that over a billion plastic bags are used each day in the United States," she said. She wanted people to stop using plastic bags. She wanted people to switch to reusable bags.

Jane Goodall is just one of many people who have used letters to make their voices heard. You can make your voice heard, too, through a letter. In this book, you will learn how.

there skiing while | but as the years progressed, my | up th
cing harmful fo | knees began to tolerate skiing | reduc
sure to our aging p. | less and less. | press

Sand   As a physical therapist for

ld hit bumps of an; | second thought about donning | woul
the bullet and b | my skis the next morning. The | I bit

Tools Writers Use

A Strong Ending

Persuasive texts cause readers to think, feel, or both. A strong ending is one tool writers use to meet this goal. Many persuasive texts end with an admonition, or rebuke. A rebuke says, "This is your problem, too, and we can do something about it. Doing nothing is not acceptable." Another type of persuasive ending works on the reader's emotions. These endings remind the reader of past events and ask the reader to make connections to the issue.

ntain with them. F | skiing apparatus biomechanical- | moun
as always been a g | ly reduces the pressure on the | ha
port! | knee joints and transfers the | ily sp

Clean Up City Park!

Dear Mayor,

Have you gone to City Park lately? Well, I have. I go there every Tuesday afternoon for baseball practice, and I have a game there every Saturday. Believe me when I tell you that City Park is a mess. The baseball fields need repair. Trash is all over the ground. Garbage is floating in the lake. You would be **heartbroken** to see what has happened to the park. It used to be so nice. If something isn't done, no one will want to go there anymore.

My dad says that City Park used to be beautiful. When he was growing up, his family spent every weekend in the park. People would swim, fish, and have picnics. Everyone loved to go there. I wish it were beautiful today. But now the park is a dump!

First of all, the baseball fields are dangerous. I know this because I am on a team. The grass is really high. One player on my team actually hurt his knee. He tripped on a weed while he was trying to catch a ball in the outfield. We lost the game, and he couldn't play for two weeks. My dad told me, "If they don't fix those fields, you're not playing anymore." He is not the only parent who is upset. The parents of my teammates are worried, too. Anyone who cares about the kids in our town should be **disturbed** about this situation.

City Lake is in awful shape, too. The lake is filled with garbage. One reason is that there are no garbage cans. Instead, a sign tells people to take home all their garbage. Unfortunately, many people don't obey the sign. I know this for a fact because my dad and I witnessed them last Sunday. We were sitting on a park bench watching the people. Some of them did take their trash when they left the park, but others did not! We saw two teenagers throw soft-drink cans into the lake. I saw a little kid drop his candy wrapper. A man and woman left a plastic bag of garbage under a tree. It was a real shame!

Here is the picture I took of City Lake. Look at all the garbage!

Then my dad and I took a walk around the lake. My dad told me that he used to swim in City Lake. Now, nobody would think of swimming there! I certainly wouldn't. Dad said that when he was a boy, he fished in that lake. I've never fished, but I would love to. I think it would be so much fun to fish in City Lake. I bet lots of kids my age would like to fish there. But no one fishes there now. The water is brown. You can see garbage floating in it. The trash is probably killing all the fish. When you look at the picture I took of the lake, I'm sure you will feel as **disgusted** as I do.

If we don't do something about City Park, no one will want to go there anymore. I would like City Park to be cleaned up. My dad explained why the city can't afford to take care of the park right now. The economy is bad. Many people are out of work. They can't pay their taxes to the city, and that means the city can't pay for park services. But that's no excuse to abandon our park. We can find another way. If the city can't pay people to keep the park clean, then we should get volunteers to do it.

I propose that our city organize a park cleanup once a month. Volunteers could work in teams. They would pick up trash. They would cut the grass. I think people would volunteer if they knew how important this is.

We could put up posters around the town to advertise the cleanup effort. The posters would ask for volunteers. My baseball team and I would make posters. We know other baseball and soccer teams that would help, too. Schoolchildren could also make posters. Then parents would get involved. They will want to make the park safe and clean for their kids.

Spring is here, Mr. Mayor. Kids want to play in the park. Families want a place to have picnics. As the leader of our city, you have the power to do something. How do you feel knowing that people have no clean, safe park? Wouldn't you feel satisfied knowing you had done something to help? Please think about my plan. I am ready to get into action— and so are my teammates.

Sincerely,

Jason Bolton

Understand the Letter
- Who is the writer of this letter? What does his letter tell you about him?
- What opinions does the writer express about the condition of the park? Find examples in the text.
- What do you think of the writer's plan to have volunteers clean up the park? Do you think the plan could work? Why or why not?

Analyze the Tools Writers Use: A Strong Ending
- What does this ending ask the reader to think about?
- What type of ending does this letter have? (rebuke or emotional)
- Which sentences support your answer to the second question?

Focus on Words: Words That Describe the Writer's Point of View
In this letter, the writer uses words to make the reader feel certain emotions. For example, in the first paragraph he describes the condition of the park and then says, "You would be heartbroken . . ." He is telling the reader how to feel about the situation. Find other emotion words. Make a chart similar to the chart below. Define each word and think about why the writer used it.

Emotion Words

Page	Word	Dictionary Definition	Why is it an effective word choice?
7	heartbroken		
7	disturbed		
9	disgusted		

Ride Bikes, Not Cars!

Dear Citizens of Fair Hills,

Have you looked around our town lately? The roads are clogged with cars and vans. The air smells bad. More car accidents happen every year. I am unhappy and **distressed** about our quality of life. You should be, too.

Are you part of the problem? Please ask yourself these questions:

- Do I live in town?
- Do I own a car?
- Do I use my car when I could be riding a bike?

If you answered yes to these questions, then I need your help. I know that you probably care about our town as much as I do. I know that if you understood the problem, you would want to make it better. So let me share some facts with you.

In 1998, our elementary school had one crossing guard. By 2008, the school had four crossing guards! That is because streets that were once safe are not safe  anymore. They are so crowded with cars that children cannot cross the streets alone.

In 1998, two children in our town were killed in car accidents. In 2008, that number jumped to six. That is a 300% increase! I think you will agree that even one child's death is too many!

In 1998, fifteen children went to our hospital with serious asthma attacks. Last year, that number was thirty-six. Experts say that dirty air can make asthma worse. Our air quality has never been so bad.

A group of students at my high school use simple instruments to measure the carbon, or soot, in our town's air. Lena Rodriguez, their science teacher, told me, "We have been taking readings for five years. The carbon content of the air has increased almost ten percent in that time."

Four years ago, our town knew that something had to be done. That is why the town built many bike paths on the roads. The town wanted more people to ride bikes instead of driving cars. But town sources told me that the number of people riding bikes has gone up less than three percent.

Come on, people. We can't be **apathetic** anymore. We have to start caring and get into action. This is our town. We're all **responsible** for what happens to it. Let's get out from behind the wheels and climb on our bikes. It's fun. It's good exercise, and it's better for our town.

Matthew Benjamin
High School Senior

Understand the Letter

- From reading his letter, what can you tell about the writer?
- Who is the writer speaking to in the letter? Does the writer know his audience personally? How can you tell?
- Why do you think the writer sent his letter to a newspaper?

Analyze the Tools Writers Use: A Strong Ending

- What does this ending ask the reader to think about?
- What type of ending does this letter have? (rebuke or emotional)
- Which sentences support your answer to the second question?

Focus on Words: Words That Describe the Writer's Point of View

Below are some strong emotion words from the letter. Make a chart similar to the chart below. Define each word and think about why the writer used it.

Emotion Words

Page	Word	Dictionary Definition	Why is it an effective word choice?
12	distressed		
14	apathetic		
14	responsible		

We Need New Playground Equipment!

Dear Principal Deets,

Do you remember when you were ten years old? Were you like most kids who get excited when they see a really cool playground? Do you remember how awesome it felt to swing up high, close your eyes, and pretend you were flying? Did you ever climb to the top of the monkey bars (even if you were secretly a little terrified like I sometimes am)?

Personally, my favorite thing to do on a playground is go down the slide. I like really tall slides. I like to climb to the top and zoom down at top speed. That is just the greatest feeling! I find that the best slides are metal and very smooth. You can go down them very fast.

The writer wants her reader to remember that playgrounds are fun. She describes what it feels like to be a ten-year-old kid on a playground. She would like the reader to think about playgrounds from her point of view.

Playgrounds are very important to ten-year-old kids. And they are necessary for our health, too. Kids like me spend most of our day sitting at a desk working very hard. We can't move around very much. We have to hold in all our energy. Our teachers don't like it when we get up and walk around. They want us to pay attention. I understand how they feel, too. If I were a teacher, I would want my students to pay attention to me. But sometimes that is very hard. Do you remember how hard that was sometimes?

When you were my age, did you ever stare out your classroom window and think, "I wish it were time for recess?" I do that, too. Don't get me wrong; most of the time I pay attention. But once in a while, I do stare out at the playground. And what I see is a **disappointment** to any kid who loves to swing, climb, or slide. That's because our school's playground doesn't have much equipment. There are only two swings. Kids have to wait in a long line to get on them. The monkey bars are not very big. And the slide isn't very fast. This is because the chute has so many dents in it. The seesaws give you splinters.

Notice that the writer describes the condition of the school's playground in great detail. She wants to support her position that the school needs new equipment.

There used to be a basketball hoop, but the hoop is gone. This equipment must be thirty years old. My dad went to the same elementary school, and he told me the same slide was there when he was a boy. Admit it, Principal Deets: It is time for new playground equipment!

I know that new playground equipment will cost money, but I'm sure you could convince the PTA to hold a fundraiser. They purchased new science lab equipment last year after you explained how important it was to our curriculum. They also got new computers for the library.

Here are some things you could tell the PTA.

1. Every other school in our town has a better playground than we do. I took pictures of them, which I have enclosed with this letter. You can share these with the PTA. If they compare our playground to the others, they will **sympathize** and get into action.

This writer offers photographs as evidence. She hopes that the photographs will support her position that the school needs new equipment.

18

2. Most experts agree that children my age should get between 60 and 90 minutes of exercise per day. One expert I saw on TV said exercise is "food for the brain." We don't have gym every day at school. We have to get some of our exercise at recess. Kids are supposed to get different kinds of exercise, too. It's not enough to run around. We also need to build our strength and flexibility. We do this when we climb on bars, pump our legs on a swing, and go up and down a slide. On our playground, most kids just stand around and talk. There is not enough to do. This fact should spark **concern** in the entire PTA.

3. There is a serious diabetes problem in our country. Children who don't get enough exercise gain weight. When you weigh too much, you can get diabetes. If the PTA improved the playground, they might save some kids from that disease. They could save some lives. They could also help kids feel better about themselves.

The writer gives facts about why students need new playground equipment. She provides more than one argument to support her position. She knows that different people are convinced by different arguments.

19

This writer also appeals to her audience's emotions. She suggests that the PTA would be making the lives of children better. She assumes they would want to do this.

These reasons alone should make you go to the PTA. But there's another reason, too. You were once a kid, so you know how we feel. And you are our school leader. We depend on you. We know you care about us and what is best for us. New playground equipment will be good for us in many ways.

Sincerely,

Amanda Lewis

We need a playground like this!

Understand the Letter

- Could you understand how this writer feels about her school playground?
- How did she help you understand her point of view?

Analyze the Tools Writers Use: A Strong Ending

- What does this ending ask the reader to think about?
- What type of ending does this letter have? (rebuke or emotional)
- Which sentences support your answer to the second question?

Focus on Words: Words That Describe the Writer's Point of View

Below are some strong emotion words from the letter. Make a chart similar to the chart below. Define each word and think about why the writer used it.

Emotion Words

Page	Word	Dictionary Definition	Why is it an effective word choice?
17	disappointment		
18	sympathize		
19	concern		

How does an author write a

Persuasive Letter?

Reread "We Need New Playground Equipment!" and think about what Amanda did to write this letter. How did she state her position? How did she support it effectively?

1. Choose a Problem to Write About

In a persuasive letter, the writer usually wants to talk about a problem. In this letter, the problem was the terrible condition of the school's playground equipment.

2. Identify Your Audience

The audience is the reader you are writing to. This is whom you need to convince. A writer must present facts and reasons that will convince her audience. The audience for this letter is the school principal. Amanda wrote to the principal because she knows that he can take her problem to the school PTA (Parent Teacher Association).

Problem	The school needs new playground equipment.
Audience	Mr. Deets, the school principal
Supporting Facts & Examples	• The equipment is old and in bad shape. • Every other school has better equipment. • Kids need playgrounds to get proper exercise. • Exercising can save lives and prevent diseases like diabetes.
Solution	Ask the PTA to hold a fundraiser for new playground equipment.
Ending	Appeals to the reader's emotions; asks the reader to think back to when he was a child

here skiing while but as the years progressed, my up th
cing harmful fo knees began to tolerate skiing reduc
sure to our aging p less and less. press

3. Brainstorm Facts and Examples to Support Your Position

Writers of persuasive letters support their positions with:
- facts (information that can be proven)
- concrete examples (things they have done, heard, or seen)
- supporting evidence (such as photographs)

4. Provide a Solution to the Problem and a Strong Ending

A writer may provide one or more solutions. In this letter, Amanda gave many reasons why the school should have new playground equipment. Amanda gave supporting facts and examples to convince the principal.

Kee

I
nd l
years
enni
skiin
loss
Fo
ryin
becau
go).
becar
voule
bit
nstar
assle
its a
I
noun
till c
ki e
GRE
m o
he bo
grand
nd i
moun

GLOSSARY

apathetic   (a-puh-THEH-tik) uninterested (page 14)

concern   (kun-SERN) worry (page 19)

disappointment   (dis-uh-POINT-ment) regret (page 17)

disgusted   (dih-SKUS-ted) sickened (page 9)

distressed   (dih-STREST) upset (page 12)

disturbed   (dih-STERBD) troubled (page 7)

heartbroken   (HART-broh-ken) saddened; without hope (page 7)

responsible   (rih-SPAHN-suh-bul) in charge (page 14)

sympathize   (SIM-puh-thize) to have the same feeling or belief as someone else (page 18)